WO

FOR

UNTAMED

By

GLENNON

DOYLE

LIGHT BOOKS

Table of Contents

HOW TO USE THIS WORKBOOK

Glennon Doyle is a mother, writer, as well as a public speaker. She is also a philanthropist who has coordinated her team in attending to pressing issues. Untamed is Glennon's second book, her first being "Love Memoir". She talks about her new relationship status; she divorced her husband, Craig, and marries a woman she meets in a writer's conference, Abby. This news surprises her fans, and everyone, because she is a Christian. But Glennon admits that it is the God in her that approves of her, therefore, she would not have to fear any man or try to make them approve of her.

The guides in this workbook are simplified and well explained for readers to learn how they can discover themselves, accept themselves, and love themselves for whom they are. The action steps will set the readers on the track of aligning with lessons of this workbook. The readers must have understood this workbook and found it valuable by providing answers to the questions in it.

Prologue: Cheetah

Two summers ago, the author and her wife took their daughters out to the zoo, where they watched an event tagged "Cheetah Run." There they met Minnie, a yellow Labrador retriever, and Tabitha, a cheetah, tamed from birth to believe she is a dog. The two were raised alongside each other, so Tabitha had learned to mimic whatever Minnie did.

That was the trick they used to get Tabitha to chase a bunny for the price of a steak.

After the run and back into the cage, Glennon understood what Tabitha felt as she paced the field, stalking her periphery and tracing the boundaries the fence created. Tabitha had probably been feeling restless, knowing there was some life better than the one she was living but was forced to be grateful and think it crazy to long for what doesn't exist, even when it did.

Lessons and Takeaways
1. Most times, we resign to normal life because we feel we should be contented with what we have.
2. Keep reaching for your dreams, even if they seem impossible.
3. There will be a nudge to tell you that you can do better than this.

Questions
1. The author felt comfortable at the zoo.

   Yes [ ]

   No [ ]

2. The author is a man

Yes [ ]

No [ ]

3. Is the author's story familiar with Tabitha?

Yes [ ]

No [ ]

4. Is Tabitha happy with her current situation?

Yes [ ]

No [ ]

5. Did Tabitha turn wild again, as Tish said?

Yes [ ]

No [ ]

6. Why does Tabitha run when her cage is opened?

_____

_____

_____

_____

_____

_____

_____

7. Why does the author compare herself with Tabitha?

_____

_____

_____

_____

_____

_____

_____

Action Steps

1. Evaluate your life. Have you always been shutting down your dreams?

2. Thinking about the situation is the first step in tackling the problem.

3. Take a conscious step to effect change. Do not just talk about it.

Part One: Caged

Sparks

One Sunday, much later, after Glennon fell in love with a woman while still married to the father of her three children. That woman, Abby, proposed to her. Earlier that day, Abby had driven to her parents' home to share her plan with them.

Her mother confessed that she hadn't seen her that alive since ten. Her research showed that the age of ten is when the internalization of the norms the world presents to children occurs. It was the age when girls and boys hide who they are to be what is expected of them.

It was at that age, Glennon became bulimic. Bulimia was the mechanism she used to express her anger and fury. It was the one time she chose not to comply with the set rules. She would binge eat and then purge it out. She thought the bulimia meant she was crazy.

But now, she realized that it didn't. Before, she was just a caged girl. And Abby was the first choice she had made without being trained to choose. Choosing her was Glennon's first original idea after walking away from the cage.

Apples

When Glennon was ten years old, she frequented CCDs at the navy Catholic Church on Wednesday nights along with twenty other children.

That Wednesday, her CCD teacher, an accountant, and a classmate's mom, told them to sit on the carpet in front of her chair as she tells the story of how God made people.

She began with how Adam was lonely and stressed, tendering the garden God placed him in. Hence, God made a woman out of him. And that woman was who tricked him into eating the apple from the tree of knowledge which God had told them to stay away from. As soon as they did, they knew shame for the first time and tried to hide from God, which was a futile attempt. God cursed them. Hence, suffering existed because of the sin to know more than we were supposed to know.

Blow jobs

Glennon and her husband started seeing a therapist after he admitted that he was sleeping with other women.

That day, she asked to see her alone. Calming herself from the excitement to blurt out everything she wanted to say, Glennon told her that she had fallen in love with a woman.

The therapist took a moment to gather herself, expressing her shock as her mouth fell open. She started pointing out all the reasons why Glennon should stop herself.

Glennon replied that it felt different. She told the therapist that she could never sleep with her husband, going further to explain how less alive she felt when they had sex. And with tears pouring from her eyes, she practically begged for her approval.

The therapist suggested giving him blow jobs instead, since most women found it less intimate.

Directions

Glennon's children believe that the shower is a magical portal of ideas. She had to explain to the youngest recently that it was because, in the shower, they did more thinking.

In a bid to steal back her expensive shampoo from that same child, Glennon opened the shower curtain and noticed the empty bottles littering the tub's edge. On the right were a collection of bottles colored red, white, and blue. The ones on the left were pink and purple.

Grabbing a bottle from the right, which was her son's side, she noticed the words imprinted on it resembled barking orders. Unlike the bottle from the girl's side, which had a list of verbs a girl should be.

The author felt true, transported back in time. Even in the twenty-first century, boys and girls are still told what they should and shouldn't be. They, being vast to fit into the rigid bottles, might lose themselves m trying to.

Polar bears

Several years ago, Glennon was called to a situation at school where her daughter Tish couldn't get over the fact that the polar bears were losing their homes and food sources because of the melting ice caps.

It was during a discussion about wildlife where Tish's teacher showed a photo of a dying polar bear to buttress her point.

But unlike other students, Tish absorbed the reality of what global warming was causing to the animals. For the next month, polar bears were at the top of the list in Tish priority. Posters of polar bears were papered on Tish's wall, Glennon sponsored four polar bears online and eventually got tired with the talk to polar bears at every event mentionable.

Glennon did everything to get Tish to forget, but none worked.

One night, after tucking Tish to bed and moments before Glennon could close the door behind her, Tish murmured how nobody cared about the polar bears. And that soon, no one would care about the humans as well. It was then Glennon realized Tish wasn't crazy to be heartbroken over the polar bears. It was the rest of us that were crazy not to be.

Tish sensitivity to things made her pay attention to how wrong the effect of global warming was. In most cultures, people as sensitive as Tish are identified and set aside as shamans, medicine people, poets, and clergy. This was because, in the real world, people like her were often dismissed because, according to everybody else, people like her held them back.

Tick marks

The homecoming court is High School Fashion Week, comprising of the ten most popular students in each grade who get to dress up and perform homecoming parades. Each year, during English class,

11

ballots are passed to vote the same set of golden ones who should ascend to court. It is usually an obvious choice right from the beginning.

The ten golden ones usually stood in a closed circle. Their job was to ignore the rest of the other students, who then judge themselves by the standard they set. Glennon wasn't a golden one, but occasionally, she gets let in on what they do. She gets invited to their parties or to stand with them at football games, which she realized wasn't because they wanted to socialize with her. It was because they needed her presence to feel golden. It made her feel uncomfortable, but the thought of what people outside the circle perceived to be happening made her pretend.

By mid-September, ballots got cast, and as a student in government class, she and her friend, Lisa, got to count the votes. Lisa's job was to pull out the names and call them aloud while Glennon tallied them. Glennon got nominated, but as the ballot box neared empty, she makes two more marks next to her name when she was sure Lisa wasn't looking. After counting the votes, she got nominated to ascend the court.

Glennon had never told anyone other than her wife that she committed high school voter fraud to become a golden girl. What made it unforgiving was the desperation she had felt enough to cheat even though knowing how uncool it was. She realized that she had done and denied several things trying to attain some standard.

Algorithms

Several months after Glennon found out about her husband's infidelity, she became an indecisive woman. The counselor at her children's school told her that she needed to find herself for the sake of her children.

So, she went into polls and research, calling her friends to know if they would know what to do. Next, she began researching, reading every article she could find about infidelity, divorce, and children. What followed was turning to the World Wide Web with searches on what she could do with her life.

Gatherings

Unable to keep herself from being in the family room as her seventeen-year-old son, Chase, and his friends were watching TV, Glennon stood at the door to peek at them. The boys were on the couch while her little daughters perched at the feet of the older girls.

As an excuse, when Chase noticed her, she asked if anybody was hungry. The boys, with their faces glued to the TV, agreed. The girls scanned each other's faces first, for an approval or a somewhat consensus before a representative replied that they weren't. While the boys looked inside themselves, the girls looked outside themselves.

We live hungry because we forgot how to know the moment we learn how to please.

Rules

Glennon's friend, Ashley, took her first hot yoga class recently. Ashley was already sweating before the class began. The instructor had come in confidently and told the class that no matter how they felt later, they shouldn't leave. It was going to get hot, but they had to be strong because that was the work.

The class started, and soon enough, Ashley became light-headed and sick. She felt desperate to leave the room, but she did not. For ninety minutes, she felt like she was close to hyperventilating. After the instructor ended the class, she rushed out of the room with a hand over her mouth till she got to the bathroom. There, she threw the door open and vomited. While she was wiping her puke from the wall, sink, and floor with a paper towel, she questioned herself why she didn't leave even though the door wasn't locked.

Dragons

The author says that she was gifted a snow globe that had a red dragon inside when she was little. She was usually scared at night that the dragon would attack her. So, one night, she kept the globe as far away as possible from her bedside.

Her friend, Megan, is an alcohol and drug addict and felt disappointed; she was old enough to get married but didn't want to. But she did get married so that she would not disappoint people who expect her to. But her situation worsened. She kept running away from the real issue. As humans, we are like snow globes; we keep trying to avoid the real issues we face. The author has been like this, hiding from her secret; her love for women.

Arms

Glennon tells how she gets sick of all her travels because of her book authorship. She must keep traveling and stand before many people on several stages, talking and writing more about her writings. After her first book, LOVE MEMOIR, she got hit with the news that her husband had been sleeping around with other women even after they got married. She was broken and confused about how to go about it. She thought of trying to tell a comeback story, saying that the whole challenge plays out to her redemption in the end. But it just doesn't come to play that easy.

She then went to this meeting of writers and meets Abby. She felt that she connected well with this woman and feels alive just thinking about her.

Lesson and Takeaways
1. Keeping our problems safe but a little bit distant doesn't destroy the problems.
2. Motivating others can be very challenging, but it has to be done.
3. We are programmed to stick to rules.

Questions
1. Rules work best on the male than female.

   Yes [ ]

   No [ ]

2. Megan solved her problem.

Yes [ ]

No [ ]

3. Megan became indecisive

Yes [ ]

No [ ]

4. Glennon is not sick of her travels.

Yes [ ]

No [ ]

5. Was Tish's sensitivity, right?

Yes [ ]

No [ ]

6. Why did Glennon want to discourage Tish from her sensitivity?

_____

_____

_____

_____

_____

_____

_____

7. How did Glennon feel about her winning the election?

_____

_____

_____

_____

_____

_____

_____

Action Steps

1. Take the right steps boldly when you feel it's the right time.

2. Get rid of problems once and for all.

3. Accept that you're not perfect and move on.

Part Two: Keys

Glenn's bulimia at childhood progressed into alcoholism and drug-use. She became pregnant at twenty-six and then began evaluating her life. She knew that she felt a burning desire to do something inside of her, but she was amazed at the fact that a smile on her face would be mistaken for having a gentle inside.

Her boiling point was when Abby entered her life, and she could express all the desires she felt inside. She felt the freedom to be who she believes that she is. So, she could reconstruct her life and be who she thinks she really is.

Feel

Key One: Feel It All

On day six of her sobriety meeting, she told the people there her story. A woman walked to her and told her that it was okay to feel what she felt. Glennon felt that what was wrong with her was deeper than the alcoholism and she didn't know how to feel right. The woman told her that she was not doing life wrong, and that feelings were for feeling. The secret was that she was doing it right and that was why it hurt.

She didn't know before that she was supposed to feel every feeling. She felt that only the happy feeling should be felt and the sad ones should be ignored, deflected or hidden.

After that meeting, things changed, she would feel every feeling, even if it was fear. She learnt not to be afraid of fear or pain. She was like the burning bush, and she could burn and still be alive.

The second lesson was that she can use pain to become. She would continue to become only if she learnt to stop extinguishing herself. It is the fire that would turn her to gold. Life is first the pain, then the waiting, then the rising. The suffering comes when we are trying to resurrect without going through the crucifixion first.

Know

Key Two: Be Still and Know

Several years ago, Glennon was restless and could not sleep, so she searched the internet for answers. She stared at the question she just asked Google and wondered why she trusted everyone except herself. Looking distressingly at all the opinions from various search results, she figured out that it was impossible to please the world. But she so mush wanted to push herself away from having to always the world of differing opinions. She needed to live her life.

She got a card from a friend, on it were typed, "BE STILL AND KNOW". It never occurred to her before that if she could just be still, that she would know. The knowing was not on the internet or with anyone. It was with her. She just needed to be still.

Since then, she practices this and comes into the realm of knowing.

Imagine

Key Three: Dare to Imagine

When she got pregnant at twenty-six, looking at her life with the present situation was so overwhelming. Then at forty, with a husband, three kids, and writing, she fell in love with a woman. It all seems opposing, but just as life chose her at twenty-six to handle the pregnancy. She feels it chose her at forty too, when she fell in love with Abby. Or it is probably her imagination telling her that life was far more than she had lived. Glennon writes that she had learned to live by faith.

Her idea of faith is that it is the belief in the unseen order of things. There are two orders; the visible and unseen. Tabitha was born into captivity. The only order she knew was the visible order of being caged and bored. Tabitha never knew the wild, but it was in her. She felt the unseen order nudging her.

Revolutionaries talk from the unseen order. They have ignited their imagination and plan from the unseen order inside the.

Glennon's job is to listen to women deeply. Many of them feel their present live is not the ideal. They say, "Not this". But they need to move from, "Not this" to "This instead". And this is only by relearning the soul's native language and living from the truest version of ourselves that we imagine.

Let It Burn

Key Four: Build and Burn

Destruction is essential to construction. Glennon says that we must decide if the truth inside us can burn a belief, a family structure, a business, a religion, an industry-it should have become ashes yesterday.

The author has had to lose what seemed good enough to accept the truest version of herself. The memos she had received form the world on how to run her life spoke about being selfless. But she has neglected that. Sure, women being selfless makes for an efficient world, but it doesn't make for a true, and beautiful world.

Glennon vowed not to abandon herself any longer, she wrote herself a new memo about what it means to have strong faith. She knows that she is human and perpetually becoming. And her entire life will be a million deaths and rebirths.

Lesson and Takeaways
1. It is best to acknowledge all feelings as worth feeling.
2. Being silent and connecting with our inside will help us with the answers we seek.
3. Destruction must take place for any construction to happen

Questions
1. Glennon's job is to listen deeply to women

   Yes [ ]

   No [ ]

2. It is best not to feel anything

   Yes [ ]

   No [ ]

3. Destruction comes before construction

    Yes [ ]

    No [ ]

4. Knowing comes from the inside

    Yes [ ]

    No [ ]

5. It is best to be afraid of pain

    Yes [ ]

    No [ ]

6. How can you reconnect with yourself on the inside?

    _____
    _____
    _____
    _____
    _____
    _____
    _____

7. What do you think Glennon means when she says,"…a million deaths and rebirths"?

    _____
    _____
    _____
    _____
    _____
    _____
    _____

Action Steps

1. Take 25 minutes off every day to connect with yourself.

2. Have the courage to lose. It is part of winning.

3. Do not be lost in pain. Grow through it.

Part Three: Free

Aches

Glennon was introduced to the Ache by a therapist. The Ache constantly remains her of essential facts of life. She looks for all means to eliminate the Ache, by covering it up with her bulimia, and then booze. So, by the time she was twenty-five, she had been arrested repeatedly and was very sick. But amidst all these, what she felt like she wanted to be a mother.

Having to say goodbye to her dying grandmother and feel so close to her new born niece, she feels the Ache telling her that," This will pass; stay close".

Ghosts

When she was sixteen, he imagines there was a perfect human woman somewhere, who was always haunting her. In her thirties, she lost that belief and accepted that she was a mess. But she still believed in that perfect human woman. The problem is that she lived in defiance of perfection not in pursuit of it.

Glennon wrote that she was born a little broken in her first memoir. But looking at her life now. She is not broken. Humans hurt people and get hurt. This is the way they were designed to function. Studying all humans, she noticed that we all act this way. But humans just seem to think that the best version of themselves is the one that is perfect; not hurting others, having it all.

She got freedom when she realized that her problem isn't that she was not a good enough human, but that she is not a good enough ghost, because the perfect human woman is a ghost.

Smiles

Some Christmases go, Glennon and her sister bought four plane tickets for both their parents and them to visit Paris. She learns to forgive America in that trip. America is so new and fancy, still trying to be the "firsts" to so this or that. Paris is calm, not jumpy.

Glennon finds proof that leaders come and go, buildings are built and fall. TO her, Paris says: We are here for such a short time.

The story of Mona Lisa is also one she felt deeply about. The smile on Mona Lisa's face is a mixture of full joy and full grief. Mona Lisa is the patron saint of honesty.

Goals

When she got pregnant with Chase and stopped drinking, drugging and purging, she thought it would be a changing point in her life. That she would stop being bad and start being good. She married Chase's father, learned to cook, clean and fake orgasms. She attended church, became a writer and stuck to trending fashion. She raised tens of millions of dollars for people who were hurting. Everyone said she was a good woman. And she strove to be a better woman. But her husband's infidelity proved that being a good wife wasn't enough to keep her marriage. Being bad had almost killed her, also being good.

Adam and Keys

A few years ago, Alicia Keys, the musical artist, told everyone that she was done with makeup. A while later, Adam Levine in an interview said that he saw her putting some lipsticks on when they were filming a show together and said," Oh! I thought Alicia doesn't wear makeup". She turned around and said, "I do what the fuck I want" That's it.

Ears

Glennon raised her daughters differently. Tish is calm and wants to think about the process of doing something, but Amma is brave and doesn't seem to show that she is afraid. One time, they both went to get their ears pierced, Amma goes for both while Tish decided she didn't want her ears pierced anymore.

Glennon is not okay with the world's definition of brave if it means to ignore fear and please people anyway. She defines being brave as living from the inside out.

Sometimes, being brave means letting the crowd think you are a coward. Tish showed tremendous bravely that day, because she resisted the urge to pierce her ear to please the people around her. It is easier to give in, but it takes bravery to honor yourself when the crowd is pressuring you not to.

Glennon ends this chapter with, "To be brave is to forsake all others to be true to yourself. That is the vow of a confident girl."

Terms

Glennon met Liz at an airport. They became friends while waiting to be picked up and delivered to the same even they were to speak. The next night she took up a front seat close to the side, so she could not be seen by Liz, but she would be able to see Liz clearly. Liz was original, she spoke with gentleness and authority.

The next night, all speakers attended a fancy bouquet in a ski lodge at the top of a mountain. She then spotted Liz across the room and wanted to speak with her. But she couldn't. During the dinner, she thought about how much she liked Liz, but was sad that they wouldn't be friends. Besides she was not that good a friend. But a few weeks after the event, Liz sent her an email asking them to be friends.

So, they did become friends, and a while later, she invited her to her house. That was around the time she met Abby. She told Liz about what she was going through and felt grateful for Liz's friendship.

Erikas

Glennon tells that recently her friend, Erika, called her cellphone. But Glennon doesn't like phone calls, it gives her heart attack. She prefers texting to calling, but still doesn't let texts steal her day by having to reply them even if inconvenient. Hence, she has no friends.

Erika and the author went to the same college. Erika was a born artist. But she studies business because her mother was a corporate executive. Erika dreaded the business classes so she would turn to Glennon's dorm to paint. She finally graduated with a business degree, fell in love with a fantastic guy, sponsored him through medical school and had babies. She eventually quit her job to take care of the kids. So, one day she decided to honor her nudge to paint. She enrolled in art school and was so excited.

So, when the call came in, she picked to honor Erika's celebration. But Erika had quit school, she found it silly and selfish. This a product of the culture that enslaves women so much that they find it honorable to dismiss themselves. Right from childhood, everyone thinks to tame women. But women weren't born distrusting and fearing themselves. They convinced women to look away from themselves and be afraid, and women who are best at this disappearing act earn the highest praise: *She is so selfless*.

Beach Houses

When Glennon wrote to her community to do whatever their selves felt like doing, he got a reply from someone that was enlightening. Our surface feeling can sometimes crowd the Knowing. She has a friend who was in debt but wanted to purchase an expensive beach house. She thinks the beach house will help her spend more time with her family, which she longs for. Finally, this friend purchased a two-dollar basket in which she mandates everyone in the family to drop their phones for an hour each. This solved the problem.

Surface desires can be disastrous but our deep desires are true, wise and beautiful and in line with the Knowing. A lot of women desire a lot of things, even the blueprints of heaven are etched in the deep desires of women. What women want is good. It is dangerous, but not to women. But perhaps it could lead to a better and truer world.

Temperatures

One morning she spoke to her friend, Martha, about all the reasons she could not leave her marriage and all the reasons she could not stay. She kept going on and on, when Martha told her to stop. The answers she needed were not in her head, but in her body. Martha told her to try dropping into her body, right then, dropping lower.

Then she asked her to consider both decisions. Is she felt cold in her body when there was danger, she would leave and when she sensed warmth, she would stay. And this has continued to help her decisions in life.

Mirrors

Glennon did not admit that she was in a lonely marriage because she couldn't do what was required of her to do if she admitted it. She instead put in effort into protecting Tish who is so sensitive, with the idea meant parenting. One morning as Tish prepared for school, she asked to cut her hair like Glennon. It was at the sight of their images in the mirror together that it dawned on Glennon that Tish was fast becoming a woman. And was looking up to her as a role model.

It made Glennon ask herself that even though she believed she was staying in the marriage for Tish. Would that be the kind of marriage she wanted for her daughter?

Eyes

Sitting down on her bedroom carpet, Glennon stared straight at herself through the mirror leaning against her bedroom wall that she and Craig had found on a clearance but never got around to hang. She asked herself if her decision to martyr and abandon herself in the name of love for her children was what they really needed from her. She came to realization that she was passing down a legacy of martyrdom to her daughters which was going to be so unfair on them. She was teaching them that love was the beginning of their own life ending. But love meant emerging for the beloved, not disappearing. There and then, she decided to start seeing her children as a reason to be brave. To not settle for a life, she didn't want or less beautiful than the one she wanted for her child.

She called Abby to admit her love for her. What followed was a confession to Craig that she was done with the marriage. When he was ready, they sat down to inform the kids, giving them permission to love Abby. Heartbroken they held on to each other, crying. What followed was letting family and friends know.

Gardens

Glennon grew up knowing just the right thing to do to be a desirable woman. But didn't know what it felt to desire until she met Abby. After she ended her marriage with Craig, Glennon accompanied Abby to LA to receive an icon award from ESPN to celebrate her retirement from soccer. At that time, they hadn't touched. Throughout her flight to LA, she was excited and giddy at the thought that this was the first time she and Abby were going to be alone together for the first time.

When she stepped into Abby's hotel room to see her leaning against a desk across the room, her first thought was that Abby was her person. They hugged for a long while, shaking while taking in the fact that they were finally together. What followed they pulled away was a lock of eyes and a series of intimate moments that ended on bed.

Vows

When Glennon was pregnant with her second baby, she initially did not want to know the gender of the baby. Until she called doctor's office after an examination one day. It got her excited for Tish's arrival. She remembered thinking then that Chase calm attitude was because of her parenting skills. Tish arrival changed that. Tish was one to always express her displease. Tish's first few years involved her being always upset that at one time Glennon got fed up. That was before Glennon realized that Tish's character resembled hers. Glennon recalled that acting happy was what had almost killed her. So, she stopped desperately trying to make Tish happy.

When Glennon and Craig divorced, Tish was the one person who kept them close to the pain. She refused to act like she was over the transformation going on in the family when she wasn't. One night, Glennon had to repeatedly soothe Tish by repeatedly telling her how she would never lose her mother. But that had happened back when she thought her job as a mother was to protect Tish from the pain instead of letting her know struggle enough to be brave. After seeing her daughter come out of the struggle Glennon had placed her in with her choice to make a change in her life, she no longer believed in lying to her anymore. Glennon decided to replace the words she told Tish every night on bed to she would never lose herself.

Touch Trees

On the eighteenth year of her sobriety, Glennon watched an intriguing televised situation where the host of the show intentionally gets lost in the woods. For days, the survivor man had not eaten food in days and was out of water. Her empathy for him blinded her from distinguishing between what was happening to him and what was happening to her. Her wife had to remind her to put up the boundaries that existed before she could watch without getting attached.

The host had said that the most effective way to increase the strategy of being found in a lost situation was finding a touch tree, that one recognizable tree that ensures that would serve as the survivor's home base.

Glennon related to the fact that all through the time she had felt lost, it was because she had made a decision outside her touch tree. Even as she felt lost at that moment, she reminded herself that she wasn't in the woods and brought herself back to "reinhabit" herself. That was her own touch tree.

Buckets

Few nights ago, just when Glennon was about to fall asleep, Tish came knocking. She told her mother that she feared feeling alone, all by herself, in her body. She crawled up the bed and shared a pillow with Glennon. They stared into each other's eyes trying to find themselves, attempting to find the blurring lines that had been establishing itself ever since Tish left Glennon's body.

Glennon explained to her through metaphors that she usually felt lonely as well. She said she felt like she was a bucket of sea water wanting to mix with other buckets of sea water. She told her that perhaps, when they were born, they were poured into these buckets.

And that over time when they die, they are emptied out again. This time, mixed with other with no buckets in between.

Later when Tish had fallen asleep, Glennon whispered into her ear that she should try to stay fluid because she was the sea, not the bucket.

Attendants

In the middle of her divorce, Glennon asked her friend Liz, who didn't have kids for parenting advice. Liz likened what was happening through the divorce to the turbulence of an airplane in which it was her children's first time flying. So, she absorbed Liv's advice that she was like the flight attendant who had to look not panicky through the turbulence because she knows the plane won't go down. A friend told her that although that was right, planes do crash indeed.

A friend of Glennon's friend found out that her teenage daughter was dying of cancer. The fear that her family was crashing for real caused her to start drinking and drugging until her daughter died. The woman had chosen to jump out of the ship out of fear.

Parenthood is serving the peanuts amidst the turbulence even though fear is felt. It is taking your babies hands and telling them that what is more real than the turbulence is the fact that you are all together.

Memos

Listing the memos gotten when her parents and grandparents left the hospital, Glennon summed up the memo her generation passes across. Always shield your child and never allow anything difficult to happen to her. Even if it meant at your own expense. It was a terrible memo that made the child refuse to rise and try again whenever he falls. The memo is what prevents the child from undergoing what would make them strong people: struggle. It is what makes us the overparented and under protected generation.

The memo should be, take the child home and love her everywhere, let things happen to her but be near.

Poems

Until Chase was handed the cell phone he so much wanted, he used to draw maps and list every country in the world and write down songs and poems. Glennon worry that giving a cell phone to a child steals their boredom which is supposed to inspire creativity. When a Silicon Valley executive who played an important role in creation and proliferation of phones admitted that her kids do not have phones, Glennon realized the impact of how phones affected creativity.

She knew Chase was getting addicted to his phone but feared that taking the phone was going to leave him feeling left behind. Much later, she realized that it was a terrible reason to give when it came to curbing an excess. Finally, while out for a walk, Glennon told Chase her concerns and he admitted his addiction to it. Chase and Tish decided to give up social media and stick to texting. Parenting is knowing and doing what is necessary for your child even though it appears countercultural.

Boys

Ever since she gave birth to her daughters, she had been raising them to be feminist, by imparting a narrative on what it meant to be a woman that contrasted with the world's view. She made effort to let them know that they were human beings and had a right to express themselves in every way possible. Five years ago, after watching headlines on CNN, it dawned on her that boys were also kept in cages.

Culture has taught them to think that they can't feel any other emotion other than rage and competitiveness. And for a long while, while Glennon busied herself with her girls, she forgot she had a son who also was left to fit into culture's prescription. Until a few months ago, Glennon had let the fact that Chase was a student-athlete let him think that home was where his left-over energy was supposed to go to while out there.

Glennon's friend, Jason told him that he cried as a child in the bathroom because his tears made his parents uncomfortable. And the times he showed his vulnerability, he felt his wife pull back. Women's orientation on men are equally as well poisoned by our culture's standard of manhood causing them to withdraw when they see a man express his feelings. The truth is that whether male or female, we are human beings created with feelings. Embracing that doesn't make us less of who we are.

Talks

Glennon and Tish visited their favorite bookstore when Tish was nine. When they got inside, Tish stared at the covers of the magazines which were full of pictures of blonds, slim and scantily clad models. Glennon did not try to hurry her long, so Tish would not have to think of aspiring to be like that, so she could be acceptable. So, she built their conversation around that.

Tish understood from that conversation that magazines have an awkward picture of who women look like in reality. And this misleading concept would make them always feel defeated because they cannot attain that standard.

Glennon writes that it wasn't enough for women to have equality with men; they needed equality with each other. She wants to teach her children not to always accept the lies that the world doles out to women. She wants to teach them to be critics of the culture instead of blind consumers of it. Instead of swallowing those lies, she can train them to detect them and get angry.

Woods

Glennon's friend, Mimi told her about how her son was spending hours behind his locked bedroom door on phone. Mimi was scared to approach him or check his phone for porn. But she must do something about it, and if her son is being exposed to porn, it would be very disastrous.

Sex is not bad. It is an exciting and wonderful thing about being human. But turning to the internet for information about sex will teach these kids an awkward meaning of sex.

So, Glennon advises Mimi to have a conversation about it with her son. She may not have all the answers for the child, she just must be brave enough to trek into the woods.

Cream Cheeses

One afternoon, Glennon opened her inbox to see an email from her kid's school to provide breakfast for the athletic team. Each morning, a parent delivers full spread of bagels, cream cheese, juices, and bananas to school. She sets it up whole the children practice so that they can dine after practice.

The night before she was to make her deliveries, she received another message from one of the mothers of the children and complained about the kids not liking the flavor of cream cheese provided by some parents. So, she advised to provide five different flavors for the children.

Glennon is a cream cheese parent but she doesn't like the idea of having to spoil the kids with different flavors o cream cheeses. Having the best of everything does not necessarily make the best people. And successful parenting should include working to make sure all kids had enough, not just the kids assigned to parents.

Bases

One morning, she woke up to read the story of how babies as little as four months old were being stripped from their mother's arms, who were seeking asylum. These kids were then loaded into vans and sent without explanation to detention centers. She searched the internet repeatedly, but she was surprised by the reaction of many who believed the parents shouldn't be there in the first place.

Privilege is being born on the third base.

With all the brutal responses people had online, she got drained and had to sleep for a very long time. She woke up energized, and ready to think of a way out for these families. Glennon and Abby called the Together Rising team and started finding people who are in the position to do something about this situation.

One morning, she posted a video that was both beautiful and utterly brutal of one of these separated kids reuniting with his family. Reactions of gratitude flooded in. That afternoon, a parent walked up to her and told her that she would never imagine doing what those parents did if they knew that their children would be taken away. But that was her imagination, and she was judging them based on herself. It keeps the danger in, but it rids them of empathy and tenderness.

Islands

Glennon talks about her relationship in this chapter. Her decision to marry Abby was hard because of what everyone else thought, including her mother. It took a while before her mother was finally in on her decision to get married to a woman.

She says that it is not the cruel criticism from folks who hate us that scares us away from our Knowing; it is the quiet concern of those who love us.

But she told Abby that she was not going to spend one more second explaining herself or justifying their relationship. She was just going to live the life and when they witness it, they will know that they were okay.

Boulders

A woman, H, wrote to Glennon about loving her new born. H was rarely loved by her own mother and fears that she would not be capable of loving her child, as a mother. Glennon advises that parents love their children, but it is possible that there are boulders that interrupt the love's flow. And sometimes miracles happen and the boulder is rolled away. But for other families, the boulder remains there. H's parents had that love, but the boulder prevented it from flowing to her. Glennon says she has been an impeded river. The boulder of addiction blocked her love, and all her family felt from her was pain and absence. Then, she got her Removal, sobriety, and her love was again flowing like a river.

Glennon tells H that the miracle of grace is that she could give what she had never gotten.

Bloodbaths

During her *Love Warrior* book tour, she had revealed to audiences that she and Craig were divorcing, but she hadn't told them that she was getting married to Abby. But she felt that was right to reveal the truth about herself to them, not minding what their reactions would be. She had a choice; she could reveal her new relationship before she was ready, or she could stand in front of her readers and hide the most important thing happening in her life.

She decided to tell the world, anyway. Anything or anyone she would lose in the process of telling the truth was never hers.

In her thirties, she learned that she didn't want to have the type of pain which was inevitable, excruciating, and necessary and one where she would lose beautiful things. Writing this book, she was forty-four years and she says that she would be damned if chose that kind of pain.

So, the next morning, she woke up to post to a million people, a picture of Abby and her snuggling on their front-porch swing, her strumming a guitar, both looking directly into the camera. She then wrote that Abby and she were in love and planned to build a life together, along with the kids and their father.

Racists

The author was eleven when she started treatment for her eating disorder. Treatments in those days were taken without considering the kind of environment in which the sick person lived. People hardly consider the probability that the sickness may be due to some toxins the patient inhaled at home.

During one therapeutic session, with her parents, her father walked out of the office because the therapists asked her dad to imagine that he might be unintentionally contributing to her illness?

Decades after this incident, Donald Trump got elected as president, a friend called her and expressed her concerns about this new development. Soon, after the conversation with her friend, he had another with her daughters to give them some education about Black freedom. Reading further about Martin Luther King, she came to a point of self-evaluation. So, she decided to read every book she found bout race in America. She also filled her social media feed with activists and writers of color.

She began to learn the way her ignorance and silence had hurt other people. She felt so ashamed and exhausted because there was so much more to relearn and unlearn and so many amends to be made.

Then, she began to speak up against racism in America. White women like her would be so uncomfortable having to be told that instead of staying silence about race, they should speak up by being anti-racist. But that is because they have been so comfortable surrounded by lies all this while.

She was afraid to put down all her thoughts in a book, but she thinks the words of Maya Angelou:" Do the best you can until you know better. Then when you know better, do better."

Questions

Glennon was in a hall holding an even in the Midwest, when an old woman stood up to ask why everybody became gay suddenly. Glennon explains that there are wild mysterious forces inside humans that they have never being able to understand and re uncomfortable about not being able to comprehend them.

She further explained that someone, sometime, somewhere-for whatever courageous reason decided to finally acknowledge that fact and this has caused someone else to take it on too. And then the movement spread.

Permission Slips

Glennon writes that a fundamentalist Christian organization announced publicly that she was no longer a member of the church. But she didn't feel hurt by it, she felt that she was never with them even before.

Concessions

Recently, Abby, the kids and Glennon were all sitting on the couch watching one of their favorite family shows. The family's teenage daughter had announced that she was queer. The parents responded that they loved her no matter what.

Glennon acknowledges that the show was trying to be progressive, but the *no matter what* part felt it was not quite acceptable, but they loved her regardless. She would say the same thing if her son was caught cheating or if her daughter just robbed a bank.

What if parenting were more of asking the children about more and more of who they really were, not telling them what they should be.

Knots

For Abby

Glennon writes a note to Abby, in her imagination. She imagined that they are in a minister's office, somewhere in Texas. Abby isn't comfortable with being there, because she doesn't believe in God, but Abby still stays there with her.

She tells Abby that her heart turned away from the church to protect herself. The church told her how she was supposed to be, not what she really was. So, she did right by turning away from the church, to keep herself whole. She chose herself and God. Therefore, they came for a visit to give hope to folks in the church.

Decals

Glennon and her then husband got involved to a church, it felt like heaven, but soon she had to disagree with their motion. She felt that the church emphasized more on sexuality and gayness, instead of focusing on the foundation of the church.

She could not forget God to start trusting man. The thing that gets her is a leader who warns her not to think or question. When hate or division is being spread in religious institutions, people have three options; to either remain quiet, loudly challenge power and take their families and leave.

Glennon feels that the God memos people get as kids are carved into their hearts and everyone owes it to the world to examine what they've been taught to believe.

There was a time on Earth-like every other time on Earth-when humanity had turned against itself. A few hoarded unspeakable riches while children starved. People raped and robbed and enslaved one another for power and money. But a few stood up against this. They saw that it was all wrong. They saw that humanity's only hope was a truer, more beautiful order of things.

The salvation was in the revolutionary idea that every last one of us is free.

Girl Gods

Glennon writes her view on why she uses the pronoun "she" to refer to God. She thinks it is ridiculous to think of God as any gender, but if the expression of God as female is unimaginable to many while the expression of God as male feels perfectly acceptable-and if women continue to be undervalued and bused and controlled here on Earth, she will keep using the pronoun "she".

Conflicts

She received an email recently from an old acquaintance at the church she left. She wrote that she wants to be able to love her but because Glennon is gay, she cannot.

Glennon feels that she is caged by her beliefs. She wrote back to the woman that if the woman loved her, she would vote for who supported her, she would not be warm toward her because she feels she would rot in hell. If the woman really loved her, she would wish for her everything she wished for her family.

Glennon says that she understands the conflict the woman is going through because she had felt that way too. For a while, she thought that she was rebelling against God, but she has finally learned that it was the God in her challenging religion.

Returning to ourselves is confusing at first. Often the voices telling people who God is and what he approves of are just voices of human beings. The voices are indoctrination.

When choosing between something some one knows and something other people taught them to believe, choose what you know.

Streams

Good art originated from the desire to show yourself, not from the desire to show off. Art makes people less lonely because it always comes from the desperate center of the artist. People often tell Glennon that writing feels like a relief, and then they feel like responding to this desire with offering to tell her their story. So, she must read numerous letters every day from these people.

One night, Glennon and her sister evaluated these letters and found out what to do about it. That was when she started the Together Rising team. Looking upstream, she discovered that when she encounters anyone with a problem, she should research to find the cause of the problem. That way she can attack the right enemy.

Together Rising team help women who bury their children and go ahead to fight the politicians who are profiting from gun manufacturing and these Children's death. When they step into the gap to sustain moms who are raising families with imprisoned dads, they go upstream to dismantle the injustice of mass incarceration. They also provide shelter for and mentoring for LGBTQ homeless kids. And go upstream to renounce the religious-based bigotry, family rejection, and homo.

They help struggling veterans get the PTSD treatment they need and deserve, and we go upstream to confront the military-industrial complex, which is so zealous to send their soldiers to war and so willing to abandon them when they return.

Glennon concludes this chapter by writing that If we want to create a truer, more beautiful world, we should keep pulling folks out of the river forever.

Lies

Glennon and her friend were one day lying on the couch, marveling, crying, and laughing about all they had let burn and rebuild during the past couple years of their lives. When Glennon says," Then, I left my family". Her friend stops laughing and tells her never to say that she left her family. She didn't leave her family, she left her marriage to create her true family.

Deliveries

Glennon confesses that she is a sensitive, introverted woman. She could die for people but would not like to meet you for coffee. Which is why she became a writer, so she could stay at home alone in her pajamas, reading and writing about the importance of human connection and community.

But amidst her quiet paradise at home, there comes a doorbell. It is strange but feels like an invasion. They immediately go through the five stages of doorbell grief:

Denial: Imagining it is not happening. Denying the possibility of anyone ringing the doorbell at that moment.

Anger: Wondering why anyone would choose to come ring people's doorbell in broad daylight.

Bargaining: They would want to remain stiff; not making any move, maybe they'd go away.

Depression: Asking the question, "Why? Why them?"

Acceptance: Picking the youngest, telling him/her to go and answer the door.

It's dramatic, but the door always gets opened. Even, if Glennon was alone in the house, she would still get the door opened and hopes it is a package.

When she entered sobriety, she learnt that feelings were like hard doorbells, that send her into panic, and then leaves her with an exciting package. So, when she got quit drinking, she began to let herself feel those feelings. It scared her at first, but they did not stay there forever and certainly did not kill her.

So, when the hard feeling knocked the door, she would put on her big girl's pants and open the door.

Anger

Glennon had harbored deep anger many years after she heard about her husband's infidelity. Even though they both attended therapy, and she tried to be patient with him, the anger would remain. Her anger would fade whenever she saw him with the children, but when she had to be vulnerable to him emotionally or physically, she would feel the flow of rage in her.

One evening, she took time to notice Craig, her husband during one of her anger bouts. She noticed that he was normal, not consumed by the anger. She was the only one who felt the negative energy. This was when she decided that she would not allow herself to be angry anymore. So, whenever anger arose within her, she would ask herself questions.

She finally divorced Craig and completely forgave him. She felt the freedom at that.

Even after this, she would repeatedly get angry at Abby for trying to relax on the couch. She felt Abby was relaxing on her. She has been ingrained with the belief that resting was laziness, and laziness was disrespect. It was Glennon's choice to either continue to accept the belief or reject it.

Heartbreak

After listening to women over decades, she has realized that people's deepest fears are:

Living without finding purpose

Dying without ever finding true belonging

People run from heartbreak, they try to hide it. But heartbreaks are a part of life, and they are meant to be used as clues. The thing that breaks one's heart is the very thing they were born to help heal.

Grief

Fourteen years ago, her sister lost her marriage and was heartbroken. She grieved that loss for a long time, until one day she quit her job and went to Rwanda to help prosecute child sex offenders and return land stolen from widows. When she returned, she got married to a man who cherished her and then went ahead to build a true and beautiful family. Glennon's sister's grief, rebuilt her. Grief is like a cocoon from which we emerge new. It shatters, but it lets you obtain the pieces to rebuild.

Invaders

When Glennon began recovery, she thought her problem was that she ate, but it was clinical depression and anxiety. The depression would suck her out of herself. It felt like sinking while anxiety is a shaky hovering above, it is feeling terrified about the lack of control over anything. But Glennon is doing it; taking her life back from clinical depression and anxiety.

Five pro tips for those who live too high or too low

Take Your Damn Meds

Glennon takes Lexapro. She also advises that if anyone is judging you for having to take your meds, and they don't have a medical license, ignore them.

Keep Taking Your Damn Meds

She advises not to go off it, even if one feels alright at first.

Take Notes

Sometimes when one is feeling good, it can be hard to remember their down self. And it goes on and on. Therefore, it is better to write notes from one's down self to one's up self, and from one's up self to the down self.

Know Your Buttons

There are both "Easy" buttons and "Reset" buttons. The Easy buttons take one to fake heavens, while the Reset buttons take one to things that will make one not abandon themselves.

Remember That We Are the Best People

Glennon has come to realize that the group of people the world refers to as mentally ill re the best people in the world. And remember that these people need to come out of themselves because the world needs them, even as they need the world.

Comfort Zones

Glennon used to stay brokenhearted and sad like it was her responsibility to the world. But she decided at forty to try something new. She made this choice out of her love for herself and Abby. She may not know what this new path will lead her. But it's nice to be happy. She feels lighter, clearer, stronger and more alive. This happiness has made her children happier, but it has made the world harder to relate to. People prefer listening to a sad and lonely woman than a delighted one.

Women may encourage other women to be bold, happy, confident and powerful, but feel angry when they see women being that.

Elmer's

Glennon only reason for interest in her children's sports was because of mediocrity. She just wanted them to know enough to not be embarrassed in gym class. With zero pressure and no real learning, her girls never stayed too long in one sport.

After the divorce, Tish retreated into food for comfort and spent more time alone in her room. When Glennon brought the matter up, Abby suggested taking Tish to an elite travel soccer team. She encouraged Tish and discussed training strategies with Craig. All through, Glennon was skeptical about it. Try outs for the team lasted every night for one week and it took all Glennon not to grab her daughter's hand and take her home. By the end of the week, Tish got enlisted. It's been few years since then and Tish is now that confident person with an identity. She's an athlete now and a leader who know what and when her team mates need.

Recently, after a game in which Glennon, Abby and Craig were present to watch, Tish told them that her coach decided to nickname her Elmer because the ball stuck to her, with a happiness that gave her three parents a glow in them.

Luckies

When Glennon and Abby first fell in love, they imagined what their ideal life would be away from the obstacles keeping them apart. Abby had written a Glennon a picture-perfect morning that included the both. It was what they always brought back when things got hard. One day, after Abby organized a dinner of six including Craig, Glennon poured out hot tea and walked out to meet Abby as she stood on the dock in the home located off Gulf of Mexico that they had bought together.

As Abby turned to her, Glennon knew she recalled its resemblance to that picture she had painted that day. They sat on the dock, Glennon's back against Abby's chest watching the fish jump and the sun set. Glennon admitted that the comment on the picture she snapped of the both that evening was right. They were lucky to have each other. And it was the life they had both imagined and worked for.

Buzzes

Glennon wasn't a fan of romantic movie but then she gets a yearning right before she changes the channel. She didn't know about romantic love until she fell in love at age forty. So, at the beginning of the relationship, Glennon felt like she was as high as the time she ate hallucinogenic mushrooms with her friends in college. She felt so different and so special. To her every other person that wasn't she and Abby was just normal.

One evening as they sat on the couch, Abby told her she felt that way because it was just the beginning phase. That it was because this was her first time falling in love. That it would change to the real part, where they stop falling together and land side by side. The real part did come and it scared Glennon so much that she wrote a poem for Abby.

They were normal people now. The special feelings came often and not in its permanent state anymore. Glennon now see that they are separate colors which was beautiful because she didn't want to be lost in love. She wanted to be found in it.

Sandcastles

Women usually are defined by who they love and that is what makes them untethered and afraid. That is why they get lost when the beloved, a child to a mother or a husband to a wife, leaves their live. Women build sandcastles and live in them. Answering the questions of who they love shouldn't define them. A woman has a life on her own. She cannot live in sandcastles because the tide rises. And when it does, she must remember that she is whole with a soul of her own.

Guitars

When they were still newlyweds, Abby popped her head into Glennon's office one day to let her know of her newly found fun, hockey. It made Glennon wonder if it wouldn't hurt to have some fun as well. She recalled her dream of wanting to be a Rockstar and set up a class with a guitar tutor that offered lessons to high school kids. When she was little she used to stand in front of the mirror with a hair brush and transform into Madonna.

She admitted that learning the guitar was hard but it made her feel more human. She believed it would make her stop being bitter at the people who are happy because they love what they do.

Braids

Craig has a girlfriend. Months earlier Glennon and she decided meet. Hence, breakfast at a local restaurant was arranged. Out of topic for discussion, Glennon talked about the white teapot she was served in with such enthusiasm. The next week, Glennon received a box in the mail with two little white teapots from Craig's girlfriend.

She is nice to the kids and even braids the girls' hair. Braiding was the one thing Glennon couldn't come around doing.

The past thanksgiving morning, Glennon, Abby and the kids got up early and drove to turkey trot race downtown. Craig and his girlfriend met them there. Craig and Chase found a position in front as they approached starting line. The rest of the girls except Abby stayed behind the pack. The girls stayed together for a while when the race started but drifted apart eventually. Glennon picked up her speed the moment she sighted Craig's girlfriend jogging ahead of her, finishing the race first. The reason was to experience a personal victory that no one noticed. Few days later, Glennon called Craig up to complain about why his girlfriend was telling Tish that she loved her.

Last Christmas, Craig and his girlfriend brought a strawberry dish instead of the traditional apple pie for dinner. After taking the family's picture, Craig's girlfriend suggested that they do a crazy one which was welcomed by the children. The next day, she posted the picture online with a caption explaining how grateful she was for having them.

Glennon believes that one day, she would ask Craig's girlfriend how to braid her daughter's hair.

Seconds

When a heated argument arises between Glennon and Abby, they usually decide to take a pause and understand that they were on the same team. That they could do better since they knew better.

Glennon described herself as the spiritual director for her first marriage because of her controlling nature. She grew up believing that responsibility meant that she controlled the people she loves. Her reason was fear of how precarious life was and belief that she was smart and creative. No one can feel or see or imagine for other people.

Glennon was learning that from her wife. She had relentlessly good ideas on the things Abby would do to bring the best in her but anytime she tried to share them, Abby notices and calls her out on it. Initially Glennon thought it was a challenge and decided to try another approach. This time, she let go of the reins and expected things to fall apart.

Then she would come to the rescue and show them things worked better on her terms. She took yoga class to ease her anxiety through the period and waited for things to fall apart. And she kept waiting. Till she unlearned that control wasn't love. She is beginning to understand that love is respecting other people's feelings, trusting that they know what they really want. That her role isn't helping other people imagine their role. But asking them what they feel, know or imagine and knowing if she can support their vision.

Ideas

One night after dinner, Glennon, her sister and her husband, Abby and Craig sat around the kitchen table while the kids chased the family's dog, Honey around the family room. Suddenly, she pulled Honey to her lap and announced that she wanted to say something.

She recalled the moment eighteen years ago when she had let him know about her pregnancy. How she was planning to break up with him before she discovered it. And how she knew they didn't fit each other but it had been the right thing to be done at that time. She apologized for going through even though she knew and told him that she hoped the next thing he tries is borne from him and not imposed.

Sidelines

Abby and Craig played on the same adult league soccer team on Wednesday nights after dinner. The whole family goes to watch them on the side lines. One day, a woman pointed to the girls and asked if they were Glennon's. That started a conversation that involved Glennon trying to explain how they were all related. At the end the woman just had to blurt a 'wow.'

Abby recalled that on one early December morning, Tish had wide eyed looked at snow for the first time in her life through her nursery window and muttered 'wow.'

The people who meet their family often blurt that exact expression because of the uniqueness of their relationship, the specificity of their family, recreated and created from the insides of every one of them.

Levels

Eight years ago, Glennon had gone to a therapist asking for strategies to cope with betrayal-induced rage. The therapist had suggested yoga to assist her get back into her own body. Glennon took up the advice but wondered on her way to yoga class why she chose to live in her mind and not in her body. She later figured out that it was because felt shame and fear while in it.

The instructor walks in and the one word that sinks in was 'Be still and know.' Glennon took in those words and stayed, just as she had in her addiction, marriage, religion, pain and shame until she knew.

Sitting on a couch with other friends of hers as Ashley told them the story of the hot yoga class, she sipped a cup of coffee. Ashley made the point that the door wasn't even locked and it brought a resolution to Glennon not to ever stay again. She was sure of herself now that she would no longer suffer voluntarily or silently or for long. And she decided to send the message across to the women in the room. To help them notice with her that the sun is shining, the breeze is cool and the doors are not even locked.

Lessons and Takeaways
1. Agree to face heartbreaks, they provide clues.
2. If you decide to be happy or sad, it is your choice.
3. Girls were not born to always hide their feelings, so were boys.

Questions
1. Did Glennon reply when the old woman in the hall ask why everybody was gay suddenly?

    Yes [ ]

No [ ]

2. Glennon felt angry with Abby for relaxing

    Yes [ ]

    No [ ]

3. Did Glennon advise to neglect meds after the first doses?

    Yes [ ]

    No [ ]

4. Control is not love

    Yes [ ]

    No [ ]

5. Should women encourage themselves to be confident and powerful?

    Yes [ ]

    No [ ]

6. How can you prevent yourself from always pressing the "Easy button"?

    _____
    _____
    _____
    _____
    _____
    _____
    _____

7. How would you encourage your child to be fierce and not run away from feelings?

_____

_____

_____

_____

_____

_____

_____

Action Steps

1. Encourage joy and happiness, not sadness and loneliness.

2. Appreciate people for being sincere even if it hurts you.

3. Allow your grief to transform you into being better, not worse.

Epilogue: Human

In the author's favorite holy text, there is a poem about a group of people who really needed to know God. When they ask God, "Who are you?" He answers," I am." So, when Glennon is asked several questions about who she is, her response is "I am."

CPSIA information can be obtained
at www.ICGtesting.com
Printed in the USA
BVHW091302230321
603268BV00018B/156

9 781952 639494